The Letters That Were Never Sent

The Letters That
Were Never Sent

_ɔ_

August J. Pettigrew

ISBN: 1544995245
ISBN 13: 9781544995243

Dedication

This book is dedicated to the beautiful spirits and souls
that are addressed in *The Letters That Were Never Sent*.
Each and every one of them brought out the best pieces of me, and
I am sharing that fact with the world.
They have all been ministering angels to my life's journey.

Contents

Hello, August!

My name is August, the new beginning. There is the number, and then there is the month. Let me explain.

My birth name, Jendollu, is quite unusual. It is a combination of three syllables from my two grandmothers and my paternal great-grandmother—Jenny, Dolly, and Lou. In Cornish, Jenny means "fair" and "yielding." In Greek, Dolly is a vision. In French, Lou is famous warrior. My middle name, Bell, also from French, means beautiful or handsome. There you have it—I am a fair, yielding warrior with vision who happens to be beautiful! I doubt the origins of the names were considered when it came to naming me. I was named for women born and raised in Mississippi, south of the delta.

Long and unusual names are shortened in unplanned and unexpected ways. Unique situations, your work, your interests, or your special relationships give you yet a few more nicknames and pet names. I have many names I answer to, including my real one. I can tell in what era of my life I met you by how you address me. My names are continuing to evolve; the changes are practically seasonal. I am way past the dreaded first day of school, when the teacher might mispronounce your name, giving your classmates just what they need to pick on you for days on end. If anyone chooses to call me something appalling, the name is shut down pretty quickly as my flexibility on my name has to pass my personal scrutiny.

I am not into numerology, per se; however, the number eight has been all over my life. I am the eighth child of an eighth child, and I was born the eighth day of the eighth month (August) with eight letters to my first name. Lay an eight down on its side, and it becomes the symbol for infinity. The number is important to the card game Crazy Eights and in the game of pool.

Eight is important in the Bible too: Jesus was circumcised on the eighth day, the inner court of Ezekiel's Temple had eight steps, eight people were saved on Noah's ark, there were eight Beatitudes of Jesus, and the number eight represents resurrection and regeneration.

August is representative of so many things. The word itself has a Latin root, indicating it relates to grandeur or increase, and it is popular in German, especially as a male name meaning "majestic dignity" or "venerable." In modern-day America the word "august" has evolved to mean "respected" and "impressive." August is a summer month in the Northern Hemisphere, and in several European countries the eighth month is the holiday month for workers.

With all of that being said about the number eight and August (and I am sure there is more), it was my friend T. C. who passed along the fictional work *The Secret Life of Bees*, by Sue Monk Kidd, to me. Of course we both loved it, and after discussing it, we both realized our favorite character was August Boatright. She was so well imagined and crafted that I wanted to be her. We did have some things in common—we were independent, we had a college education, we were both teachers, and we both had a good sense of our community and the world. She used bees to explain her place in the world, whereas I often use chickens (that's another book). I cannot be August Boatright, but I can be a new and improved version of me and take some of her moxie.

My new beginning is underway, first, because I have been spiritually regenerated (again) and second, because the circumcision of my heart has been completed. There is no unforgiveness or pain being held hostage there, and my soul has been broken out of prison—the prison of everything unpleasant in my past. I am a retired public-service worker and an empty nester. I am in a new state emotionally and geographically, and I see so many new adventures ahead. This is my new beginning, my August. I am August J. Alas, one of my nicknames I choose for myself.

Dear Jesus,

It was a beautiful day when I saw you resting at Jacob's Well. The afternoon heat probably added to the need to sit and rest a minute. I was tired and hot too. As I approached the well, I quickly averted my eyes so you could not see how intently I was looking at you. There was something about you. You spoke to me anyway, when you knew I was obviously trying to avoid you. I was trying to stick with the mores and not add anything else negative to my reputation. You were trying to be kind and show grace. It is amazing, Jesus; this was a critical encounter in diversity, considering the culture and my gender.

There was so much I did not understand about myself, Jesus, but you allowed me to pour my heart out and cleanse my soul. You already knew my every sin and transgression. I had committed every sin except physical murder, and you forgave me of all of these deeds. How could I deny any of them when you saw right through me? Thank you for explaining my life to me. You broke it all down by exposing all aspects of my life to me in a brand-new way. I no longer care what any man or woman thinks of me. I no longer hide behind a fig leaf or other facade. How special—after it was all exposed, torn down, and forgiven, you healed every hurt and pain and spoke of loving me unconditionally, despite myself and my past.

Thank you for the common, everyday ground water that satisfies my physical need, and thank you for the living spiritual water that springs up a fresh well of hope in me every day since I met you. Thank you for allowing me to ask you questions and for being patient in answering my inquiries. Thank you for not ridiculing my curiosity about getting into what this new life is all about.

Thank you for enlightening me with the profound parable of reaping and sowing and sowing and reaping, and thank you for all of the beautiful gifts of life that I did not have to labor for. Thank you for the wake-up call, Jesus. I had not realized I was spiritually dead and was sleepwalking. I suddenly lack nothing in my life and have no worries; there is new peace, new joy, and abundance.

I do not have to gossip or spread rumors about you since I have met you personally. Thank you for taking the time to allow me to get to know you. I am grateful that you gave me permission to share our meeting with others everywhere I go, and even better than that, I appreciate you accepting my invitation for you to spend time with me each and every day, and as often as I need to. This acceptance has so blessed and filled my heart.

Thank you for your anointed and called sons and daughters who have dealt with me on your behalf so that I could grow in faith and love. They are truly awesome and much appreciated.

I love you, Jesus.

Dear Dr. King,

I am in awe of you! The sincere dedication and passion you demonstrated toward all human beings is phenomenal. For over thirteen years, you were active in faith and peace, trying to make the world better for all people. I wonder what you would think of today's America. I know that is a broad question, and if it were possible, I would like to hear the first thing that comes to your mind.

We have come a long way because of your good work, but we still have a long way to go. We still do not consistently love and respect each other enough. We are not genuinely open and loving. We have brand-new kinds of hatred to deal with and more technology to help us launch it more rapidly and widely around the world. It is ugly. Nevertheless, Dr. King, thank you for advancing civil rights around the world. Your speeches and sermons still resonate and make a difference to the two, three, even four generations of the people you left behind. Your written and spoken words made life-changing differences for so many. Yet some were not stirred or moved at all, making it difficult for us to unify around common causes and issues. I think our egos are too big, and we think more of self and individualism. We now have less time for each other and common issues than before.

I am also curious about your thoughts on the name change your father selected for the both of you. You were so young when the change occurred, and I have a general understanding of why. Martin Luther was a reformer, essentially one of the many things you grew up to be. Martin Luther did a lot for religious freedom and the advocating of one's free will. He greatly influenced the church and the culture of his time. I am sure your father changed both your names to announce the existence of the new person he had become. I just recently went through a similar process myself. I did not change my name; rather, I gave myself a new nickname of my own choosing, reflective of the many recent and good changes that have come about in my life. It was the conclusion (with an exclamation point!) to the transition of the new me. It reminded me of the parable: to not to put new wine in an old skin.

Growing up brings its unique set of issues to all of us. I would also like to hear your thoughts on two things from your childhood. One, did you have depression as a child, or was it one depressive episode over the loss of a loved one? The second thing, how long did you feel skeptical about Christianity? I was not a skeptic in my youth; I lacked the ability to make Christianity a priority until I did a lot more maturing, as the concept was over my head when I was a child.

Your educational résumé is also impressive. You were able to leapfrog two grades and pass a test to get you started on your secondary education as a "younger" teenager. Having seen the value of an education and pursuing a specified vocation, you became an academic star of sociology and divinity—what a good overlay to your ultimate calling.

Your tireless efforts—which opposed poverty, injustice, segregation, and violence, and promoted the right to vote, higher wages, and better treatment for all people—certainly did not go unnoticed, and they came with such a high price to your life. I might have quit after one or two arrests, but you, sir, kept going after over twenty-five arrests. I might have quit after being physically assaulted a time or two, but you, sir, were attacked at least four times. Then your house was bombed, threatening your family. Those who were against the cause and did not want to see you succeed called you a communist and did surveillance and wiretapping, trying to entrap you. They did not find what they were seeking, so they tried to blackmail you to force you into quitting. You kept soldiering on, and today we are all benefactors of your sacrifice. Thank you for the boycotts and nonviolent sit-ins that lead to the Civil Rights Act and the Voting Rights Act.

The accolades you received were well deserved. The most notable among these is that you were the youngest person to receive the Nobel Prize—not to mention the posthumous Presidential Medal of Freedom, the Congressional Gold Medal, Man of the Year, and umpteen honorary degrees. All were well deserved, as indicated by the national holiday that now celebrates your life and legacy. It was not in vain, and your legacy is active and alive today.

Dr. King, I just love you, my big brother. I appreciate all of your work and your sacrifice. Your life was worth it, and I am glad you fought the good fight and are now resting with your crown.

Dear Women of My Life,

This letter includes you if you think it includes you, and I am openly praising your place in my life. I know I would not be who I am or how I am without the fresh nuggets of wisdom you dropped in my life at one time or another. Some of you have been with me my whole life, some for over fifty years, and some just one year. There are some who were impactful but did not stay in my life long. They deposited something valuable and then moved on. The length of time is not what matters; it is the quality of the relationship and the significance it had or has in my life.

There was a very impactful poem that started circulating around 2010–11. The poem, whose author is unknown, explained how people are in your life for a reason, a season or a lifetime. I adopted this, and I live by it, because it so easily explains a lot about friendships. I have had a time or two that things changed and I did not know why. After reading this poem I was able to see plainly, and with a healthy emotional perspective, that the reason or season was over.

People come into your life for a reason, a season or a lifetime.
When you figure out which one it is,
you will know what to do for each person.
When someone is in your life for a REASON,
it is usually to meet a need you have expressed.
They have come to assist you through a difficulty;
to provide you with guidance and support;
to aid you physically, emotionally or spiritually.
They may seem like a godsend, and they are.
They are there for the reason you need them to be.

Then, without any wrongdoing on your part or at an inconvenient time,
this person will say or do something to bring the relationship to an end.
Sometimes they die. Sometimes they walk away.
Sometimes they act up and force you to take a stand.
What we must realize is that our need has been met, our desire fulfilled;
their work is done.
The prayer you sent up has been answered and now it is time to move on.

Some people come into your life for a SEASON,
because your turn has come to share, grow or learn.
They bring you an experience of peace or make you laugh.
They may teach you something you have never done.
They usually give you an unbelievable amount of joy.
Believe it. It is real. But only for a season.

LIFETIME relationships teach you lifetime lessons;
things you must build upon in order to have a solid emotional foundation.
Your job is to accept the lesson, love the person,
and put what you have learned to use in all other relationships and areas
of your life.
It is said that love is blind but friendship is clairvoyant.

— Unknown

There are some females who will tell you they are not friends with other females due to "drama." That is unfortunate, and sometimes looking in the mirror may help, giving consideration to one's upbringing or psychology. I hope those females find other positive outlets and support. I am thankful I have never had such a problem; I have always easily related to women (and to men too, but this letter is not for them). A lot of the bonding started with my mother. When I was not old enough to be left on my own, she took me along to her "girlfriends'" houses when she went to visit. They exchanged food and shared the abundance and overflow from each other's cupboards and fruit trees. They traded books and magazines. They laughed, gossiped a little, and complained about you know who: their husbands.

Thank you to all my women friends of the sisterhood who are still with me. You sweet women are from all walks and all decades of my life and come from varied ethnic groups—how lovely. I am happy our personalities and general natures mesh well. We have had some bonding and nurturing experiences, and our sisterhood is real and thriving. We are gifts to each other, and we are each other's choices. We talk openly and honestly when we hang out. We are linked by the love of God and spiritual bonding, by our vocations, by our blood, or by our common interests. Our deep sisterhood is on a rung that is higher than "friend" on that relationship ladder we have built over time. Our love, trust, and honor have us up there together, and we respect our unwritten female etiquette.

I am a girl's girl, one that is sincere and not petty. I do not covet, and I am not jealous. I am pointedly thoughtful and decent, and I wrote this letter to let you know I love you and appreciate you. Thank you for your encouragement and inspiration, which continue to guide me toward becoming the well-rounded woman I am meant to be.

Girlfriends, thank you for helping me to not overly engage in current events and other topics that are not healthy, and thank you for other activities, excursions, things, and events you brought to me that were much more fulfilling, fun, and satisfying without overindulgence.

It is my wish that we keep going, growing, loving, and having fun in the parallelism of our life and time on our intersecting paths!

Dear Mama,

Forgive me, Mama; I had an average brain. It did not mature until the average age of twenty-five, and I do believe that in many ways, there were still pieces of me that bloomed even later. By the time I took my young, wild, fun-lovin', care-free party brain off the shelf and out of the pickling jar and put it back in my head, its command center was fully functioning, and I understood more about you as a person. Shortly thereafter, I became a mother. That was when I "really" started seeing you as more than "mother." You were a woman, and now I was one too. Our common day-to-day activities were visible and were taking our relationship to a new place, a new level. We were not, and would not ever be, equals, but we now shared some of the same responsibilities and activities in our day-to-day lives. Because I recognized your fun and games, your personality, your winning ways, and your wisdom so late in my life, I can only look back and say I wish I could have gotten it sooner and spent more time knowing you and enjoying you as the wonderful woman you truly were, not as just a duty-bound, obligated attendant to house and child. You were so much more than those limiting values.

The birth of our Starla girl brought so much to the light. When she was born, the nurses wrapped her in modern-day swaddling and said, "Here, Grandma." That unique bond of mothers and daughters was being carried into another generation. I knew at that moment that Starla was going to be someone special to you, as it was your strong, capable hands that gave her the first touch of love. You're the one who told me she was a girl.

The significance of you as mama boiled down to this: no matter what I would become, you would be proud of me—proud of me, defender of me, and forever bound to me. That's what love is.

Dear Miss Val,

You met me probably when I was a toddler or preschool age. It turned out you were the mother of one of my truest, dearest, oldest friends, and you never hesitated to tell me I was special. You had something in common with my mother in that you were going to love me and be proud of me no matter what. I was special in your eyes because you noticed I always carried myself with a happy disposition. You witnessed people with special issues be drawn to me. They saw something warm and inviting in me, something that was accepting of them. You observed this and considered it a special gift long before I even considered it a part of my innate character. You saw my willingness to embrace those who were odd, unusual, or challenged. Your early observations of me would come back to me clearly when my daughter was born and there were "problems." You told me before we knew what we were dealing with that I was uniquely capable and qualified to deal with my daughter. With love and gusto, I had to dive in in unexpected ways to take care of her.

You passed from Earth's realm in 1992. I regret that you and I did not get to travel to England together to see Big Ben and the River Thames, or to sip afternoon tea in London. I am not sure you ever visited England after you came to America. It finally worked out for me—I did go to London, nineteen years later, with one of my sisters. Of course I thought of you while I was there, and about how you believed in me, which still makes my heart happy. By the way, I loved England and am so ready to visit again!

Dear Little Devil Man,

You are little because you are matchless against God. You have been for-given over seventy times seven hundred seventy-seven million times because Jesus told his friends to do so. It is amazing how you lie and deceive so natu-rally and habitually. You become clandestine and secretive after catching your victims, and before they know it, they are keeping your secrets too by be-ing loyal to your lies. You cunning little devil man, you come through like a charming white squall and leave a path of destruction, devastation, and brokenness. You leave in your wake many women, children, and friends who have to pick up tiny pieces of shards and scraps to rebuild. Rebuild they do, by grace. You could see the pain and the resonating heartache from the little to the ginormous, in all of their faces. The looks they aimed at your back had the power to kill you, but "God's grace". You were slick, but you did not get away completely like you think you did. There is *One* that sees and knows all. You cool cat, I must warn the little brothers and sisters about you and help place them on a solid foundation on which to brace themselves and be protected. I have to teach them about dignity so they won't let you wipe your feet on them. In the meantime, little devil man, you are our brother, our family, and we are stuck with you for life. We are going to keep praying for you so the *One* can help you. We love you, but not your ways.

Dear Ms. Alice Walker,

Your life looks fabulous from where I am! It has my idea of what "well-lived," "well-worked," and "well-enjoyed" mean. I hope I am right about it. You have encompassed and embraced all kinds of love and humanity in your life. Your list of accomplishments and vocations is staggering; I admire it. You are a mother, a sister, a friend to many. Some know you personally, and others, like me, know of you. I appreciate your assistance as an aid worker, a civil-rights activist, and a voter registrant. I am sure those passionate projects overlapped well with the training and experience you had as a teacher, lecturer, social worker, and other skill sets. You have completed some fantastic international travels for the sake of teaching and helping others. The list of honors and awards given to you is prodigious. One of my older sister's introduced me to some of your literary compositions years ago. It is beautiful that you had the dynamic talent to move around different genres and styles in novels, poetry, and short stories. Thank you for nearly fifty decades of literary accomplishments and writings that encourage us all to seek wholeness and equality. You modeled it and some of your fictional characters provoked it.

If I had a chance encounter with you, I would not take up too much of your time. I have narrowed down the questions I would ask:

1. After leaving your birth state of Georgia, which place did you like living in best: California, New York, or Mississippi? I was born in Mississippi, and I grew up in California. I definitely have an affinity for the South.
2. Of the forty-plus books you have authored, which one is your favorite? My favorite one is your most famous novel.
3. Aside from Zora Neal Hurston, who was influential to your writing?
4. What are you currently working on—is it work or hobbies?
5. What was or is your favorite occupation of all that you have experienced?

See, that is not a long, time-consuming list.

I will close now and wish you a good day. I just wanted to say hello and let you know I appreciate your contribution to literature and to my beautiful American life. I am also happy you found a definitive meaning for yourself as a "womanist."

Dear Ms. Maya Angelou,

My dear lady, you were a survivor! Survive you did. What did you not try in your lifetime? Poet, memoirist, sex worker, dancer, performer, streetcar conductor, journalist, activist, mother, actress in television and movies, historian, teacher, and all the other occupations that should be on this list but that I cannot recall at the moment! Once you found your lost voice and attached your power to it, there was no stopping you or holding you back. What a life—maximized in every way.

Many of your occupations were accomplished before I knew who you were. One of my older sisters introduced me to *I Know Why the Caged Bird Sings*, and I pretty much followed up on that by reading most, if not all, of your memoires, autobiographies, and poems. I also had the privilege of seeing you in person at least three times. You made the rounds on college campuses and such.

I love the confidence you carried as a statuesque, renaissance woman who was true to herself. You walked it out, wrote it out, and talked it out, so eloquently. You were sought after for convocations and lectures all over the world. You took yourself to exotic places and foreign lands, by being well-spoken and engaging. You lived in Africa, in Egypt, and you worked in Europe. You were fluent in many languages: Hebrew, Spanish, French, Fanti, and Italian. You just decided you would never quit working, learning, and loving, and I am glad about it. The life you led and the things you did are still living on and reaching far. That is your legacy! You are in the books, sister!

Ms. Angelou, you were on a mission to encourage and inspire all who would dare to engage in becoming better writers, thinkers, and citizens. I attest that the individual pursuits in that regard should never end, as per your example. I work on this every day because I do not want my brain to die. I am always learning. I do not want to go back to school; I will take an autodidactic approach to the things that interest me, and likely, I will be working and serving somehow to the day I die.

You said, "There is no greater agony than bearing an untold story inside you." I am starting by writing thank-you letters that should have been sent a long time ago to people I admire and are part of my story. I had decided to write the letters before I recalled your having said this. It is so cleansing, puri-fying, and fulfilling. And let's not forget, it is kind and considerate. I am glad that the vision, the time, and the space finally lined up so I can confidently share more of my life story and those who helped me get this far.

Thank you for your part.

Dear Chief Justice Earl Warren,

I would have loved to hear you on a college-campus lecture hall, with a dedicated hour or so for questions and answers after your talk. I wonder if you were as gifted as an orator as you were in writing. That writing that was so profound and intelligent. I would have enjoyed a cup of coffee with you following such a speaking engagement so I could pick your brain a little bit.

Like most public figures, you were both loved and hated; so many of us swing our feelings around and around and reverse who is in and who is out. You know this so well. When the president appointed you to the Supreme Court, he thought and spoke highly of you. He described you as a person he thought had ideas of politics, economy, and social justice, in a similar conservative opinion as his. But then you exercised your brain power, "interpreted the constitution with the times," and gave your legal decisions. Your opinions seemed to be more on the side of liberalism, and you empowered individual rights. The president seemed to not like you anymore and expressed it publicly. Wow! My mind is still blown when grown men in powerful positions become so childishly sulky!

I wonder if the best of your years were in our beloved California or on that other coast. Either way, you did a lot of hard, dedicated public service once you became a lawyer: as district attorney, attorney general, governor, and chief justice, and let us not forget, as an officer in the US Army during the First World War.

I would have loved to be able to chat with you about the most meaningful place, position, or thing you experienced. You know your private thoughts on what shaped you and what drove you. I know what is in the history books: mostly, how you gave a much wider berth to individuals with regard to racial integration, justice, and representation. You were involved in so many cases that changed matters of the law, and college campuses all over America cannot give instruction in that regard without the mention of you and your opinions: *Brown vs Board of Education* (1954), *Mapp* vs *Ohio* (1961), *Gideon* vs *Wainwright* (1963), *Miranda* vs *Arizona* (1966), *Loving* vs *Virginia* (1967), Watergate, "one man, one vote," and the commission on the assassination of John F. Kennedy. You were practically an entire course of study all by yourself when I was doing my undergraduate work in criminal justice. Your decisions during the 1950s and 1960s, at a time of national disobedience and civil unrest, met the duties and obligations of your position on the Court. I am almost certain you received a lot of flak from your peers.

The one thing that I would really like to hear from you directly is about the internment of Japanese people in America. I read that you considered it a "terrible mistake based on unsubstantiated fears," but is that an apology? That was three years of hell for a group of people, most of whom were born in America.

Chief, for obvious reasons, our meeting cannot take place. Just know that your impressive work history and your legal interpretation of the Constitution are still most intriguing, and I am extremely curious to know what you would think of the current climate in America. I would also like to know if you would reverse yourself on any decision you previously made that changed the rights of American citizens.

Dear Members of the Armed Forces,

You are so special to me. I appreciate all you go through on a daily basis to stay ready to serve, protect, and provide.

I was reminded of your presence recently. I was happy to be on the freeway heading to church. I had left the house early enough to be on time. My drive was going well until the traffic, which there was usually none of at this time, slowed to a crawl. I was wondering what was going on as I crept along, and I finally saw it. The last jeep had a big sign on the back: "Convoy ahead." I was able to change lanes and move a little faster. I was able to count twenty-five vehicles before I reached my exit. It was not just twenty-five-plus vehicles; it was a work force that was traveling with a whole city to be set it up in a new, remote location. I could not gauge how many more vehicles were included in the convoy, but in the middle of the line, there was the medic. Right there, I began to pray for all American service members, where ever they were, for dear God to cover each and every one and return them home safely.

Each service member has a position of incredible responsibility to each other and to the American people. You put in so much training and hard work to gain special skills. Of the many side benefits to serving, you gain health and fitness, vocational training of various kinds, and communication skills to become leaders and make requests; you keep impressive tool belts and tool kits to get the job done. You are warriors with muscles from the top of your head to the bottom of your feet. You can push it, pull it, drive it, sail it, or fly it. Your missions are many: defend, rescue, provide, deliver, provide security, police, and enforce.

Your professionalism in appearance and carriage make you ambassadors all over the world. You know your missions are never for personal gain. You do team work and look out for each other, and that camaraderie says no mission is a one-person activity. When you carry each other and lift each other up, there is no weakness.

Your communal contributions are recognized by many civilian partnerships. You are the decision makers that see us through. Your bearing, self-discipline, and responsibility for your actions is commendable.

You travel worldwide out of duty and with the utmost flexibility and adaptability. The sacrifice affects you and your family, and you do it with short notice, tenacity, and moxie. The travel and exposure to other cultures and countries further educates and prepares you for other missions and assignments. The experience will be with you for life, and I hope you will make the best of it.

In the meantime, know that you are much appreciated; I thank you for serving. Your backbone makes us Americans strong.

Dear Mrs. Roosevelt,

There was so much promise in your life from the beginning. But before you could get started, you had emotional grief to work through, at such a young age. I have seen extreme alcoholism turn into a mental-health issue, and I have seen deteriorating health conditions as well. Sadly, these two things left you an orphan, and I was not exposed to the devastation of these things until I was a young adult. Raised by relatives, you were brought up well, and despite the privilege and high society, your upbringing encouraged service to others. There were people and situations laid solidly at the foundation that kept you on the path of giving, sharing, and caring.

Like you, I went through an awkward stage, with those growing pains of learning to accept the things you could not change about yourself, learning to love yourself, and finding your assertive and confident voice. We were not alone in the struggle to figure ourselves out. Regarding those trials and tribulations, you are famously quoted all over the world, and there are probably a thousand books of "Eleanor Roosevelt quotes." One of my favorites is: "No one can make you feel inferior without your consent." It is amazing when one arrives at that realization!

Your resume is so impressive: writer, activist, teacher, mother, television-commercial actress. You championed the causes of women in society and advocated for equality, civil rights, and social reform, and I do not believe this is the complete list of your achievements! You successfully wrote newspaper columns and held press conferences over the course of twenty-seven years, surprising for someone who was a shy wallflower. You became a very public first lady of New York and of the United States and often risked your own life for the causes you were passionate about. You were literally scolded for sitting by black people on more than one occasion, and the KKK wanted you dead. Still, you went on to discuss antilynching laws, protested segregation, worked with the NAACP, and persuaded the Army Nurse Corp to admit black women. You were ahead of your time, and I thank you for all of your work and finding the platform to speak out because it helped shaped a better nation for all of us.

You were able to volunteer your time to visit wounded vets during both world wars and did a lot to aid women in voting. You remained humble through the bestowing of umpteen rewards and honorary degrees.

After you became a widow, I was amazed to see that you continued to work on several presidential commissions on the status of the American people's social needs.

Again, Mrs. Roosevelt, I just wanted to say thank you for all of your service, and for the way you conducted yourself and helped others. I like to think we could have worked together in some capacity and possibly could have been friends. I close with one of your quotes: "Friendship with one's self is all important, because without it one cannot be friends with anyone else in the world." Even though we never met, I choose to call you "friend" anyway because we have some things in common and because I stand on your shoulders because of your groundbreaking service.

Dear Miss Manners,

I am glad you are still here working hard, addressing manners and etiquette. I have some concerns, and you are free to share this letter with your friends and colleagues.

I do not understand why we are not as nice to each other as we used to be. We are tolerating so much disrespectful and rude behavior, it seems to be the acceptable new normal. The deterioration is rapid.

Please help me out and let me know if I am correct in thinking the basic pieces of politeness are still the foundation of how we address and interact with each other. Should we always be polite to each other? Should we always say, "Please," "Thank you," and "Excuse me"? Maybe I have been slacking off too, so I am starting right now in my personal effort to get better about extending these basic courtesies to everyone. Help me by joining me and getting the word out.

In my attempt to bring politeness back, I will try to speak a little softer and watch what I say. Maybe it will rub off on others and it will cause them to reciprocate. I will try to hold the door open for others and to offer up my seat, especially for the elders and the disabled. I will work on listening more intently and on being more patient by holding my tongue until it is my turn to speak.

A real irritation for me is making business and service telephone calls. Greeting the representative with courteousness is easy in the beginning, provided the hold time does not exceed, let's say, fifteen minutes. After repeating the same thing seven times with each transfer of the initial call, and having to kindly tolerate the much-exaggerated politeness, I have a hard time remaining patient. The only say-so we have over business policies and practices is to use the complaint line. I am good at that, and it is effective most of the time. I have been working on my breathing to help me stay calm in addition to helping me get better about staying on top of my patience for this one. Do you have any other suggestions?

Casual Friday has extended to casual Sunday through Saturday in and out of our workplaces and throughout our communities. Some of us wear the same thing to sacred places of worship that we wear when presenting ourselves in court, and then leave that outfit on to take the trash out and do yard work. I still have a few rules for myself in this regard. One, I would not go to a court of law to face someone in a robe with a gavel while I was wearing shorts and flip-flops. I had a lengthy vocation working in the judicial system, so this one hits a professional note with me. Respect the authority of the judge, and respect the profession. Second, I do not want to look like I have just left a gym, been out running errands, or been out to the club before stepping inside a church with the same look. I know, it can be economical to cut down on wardrobe expenses, but sometimes we still need to respect positions and places of authority and groom ourselves and look like we care when going outside the house to be around other people.

I would like to see more written thank-you notes too. I understand it takes a little time and someone may have a large number of people to address; however, this should not negate the fact that some things warrant a personal note. Anyone can put aside five minutes a day until the list is done. A little more heart and personal attention will still go far, don't you think? I still send personal notes occasionally, and I am pretty good about offering kind words and congratulations, but let me check and see if I can do better with that too.

Cell phones are everywhere! Most of us no longer consider when or where they are appropriate or not. We are so engrossed with these gadgets that we do not see people who are waiting to help us or serve us, and we do not see the eye rolls and dirty looks. I did have to back up a little here and consider the many, many more uses we have for our cell phones. Being courteous still goes back to our need to be considerate and think about the interaction we should be having with the people who are physically present around us and respecting them. Another thing about the phones of today is that we have caller ID, so we do not acknowledge wrong numbers before just hanging up in someone's face. We do not check our attitude.

Our table manners are also competing with our cell phones and iPads, other tablets, and other devices. We get up and down from the table and usually do not say, "Excuse me" when leaving the table. We look down and use elbows, reach over, and may pass something when it's asked for, without even looking up. Help us.

We are dealing with our new interventions and devices and how they help us and hurt us. They are changing every day, but we still need some manners and etiquette in how we interact with these devices and platforms. We all have individual ways of utilizing our gadgets and social media. There are some people who use Twitter, Facebook, text messages, and e-mails. I acknowledge how easy and convenient it is to reach an entire group of people, from two to two million, at one time with just a stroke of one's finger. When the situation or reason for communicating is more personal and intimate, I have adopted the rule of thumb that it will not be sent or conveyed through social media. Face-to-face communication still works, and when that cannot be accomplished, individual contact by other means may be better. We need to encourage each other to stop and think about the things we are sharing and why. We have the technology and capability to capture and report information immediately; however, we may need to pause and think about it first. Yes, I have had to discipline myself about this. I did get overinvolved and carried away. Not only was it easy, it was time-consuming and not the most productive way to use my time and talents. It also reminds me that young people are especially at risk and vulnerable with this.

Speaking of young people, I think we need to quit giving them excuses for poor communication skills. As soon as they are able to talk, good manners and etiquette need to be instilled. Let the communication with good manners and etiquette become the ground they walk on toward the platform they will stand on as adults. It is not up to one person. Let us *all* model better behavior for them. "All" has no limits, but hopefully it includes parents, care providers, babysitters, early-childhood educators, coaches, trainers, mentors, leaders, and elders—you get the point, everyone in the village and beyond.

Thank you for reading this letter and considering my top concerns about the manners and etiquette of today. Miss Manners, thank you for allowing me to partner with you on the reeducation that is so needed for our children, ourselves, and all of our loved ones.

What's Up, Coconut?

You have been around a long time. Yes, an amazingly long time. Enough to have a history of ups and downs, with myriad relationship descriptions. You remember them all, I'm sure. At times we were a single soul in one body; and at other times you were a second one of me. What a long, winding road. God's peace and blessing to you today and always: "The Lord bless you and keep you; The Lord make His face to shine upon you, And be gracious to you; The Lord lift up His countenance upon you, And give you peace" (Numbers 6:24–26, NKJV).

Dear Lydia,

We have both been in the same place at different times. Our spirits were insisting there was a truth we needed to find in order to be fulfilled. Our minds, heart, and soul took the time needed to get prepared to receive that truth when it was time. You already loved the Lord and had heard a lot about him when you were with the other women gathered by the river, working and praying. You had an open heart when you heard the message from Paul, and you knew that was the word you had been waiting for. It was no coincidence that Paul and Silas came to Philippi, and you were among the people who heard the teaching they gave.

My seeking and finding did not come in one moment like yours did. My quest needed more stimulation before my hardened head and hardened heart could be the receptacle needed for what faith would deposit there. I finally got it, and now I have been grafted into the family with Paul and Silas, like you were.

Lady Lydia, by all recorded accounts, you were a successful businesswoman, selling high-end and low-end purple cloth. You apparently had methods for the cloth and the dye that would satisfy royals and emperors, and the common people as well. It is also well known that you were a hospitable woman, offering your home as a safe place to rest and pray. There is still so much about you that is mystifying. You were a Jew, but yet you spent time by the river and in the marketplace with Hebrews and Gentiles. My lady, we are not sure of your real name, but we recognize "Lydia" as your ethnicon. What I do know about you is inspiring and prompted me to write you a short letter to tell you so.

I am about to go into the marketplace and work with my hands and mind, like you did. Thank you for demonstrating how it could be done. By faith, I pray to meet great success like you did. I will also share the blessings and my home as a safe place to rest and pray. It will be a welcoming time for support after doing my civic duties around town.

Dear Queen Esther,

You are a great historical gift and role model! You had one year of formal training to enter the contest and interview of your life. I have had a much longer training period and preparation by many women, friends, sisters, coaches, and mentors to get me ready. They certainly helped open my eyes and pointed me toward the right pathway. Some were making deposits without even knowing it. Through it all, I have finally learned to value myself like God values me, and I have learned to ask Him what He wants of me. Remember when you had that sudden revelation and new perspective? Thank you for reminding me to first calm down before fasting and praying. These two steps of preparation have become my standard practice for challenges, thanks to you. This steadies me and readies me to stand on the platform and make my petition.

Queen Esther, thank you for acknowledging the time, place, and purpose for why you wore born. It was realized in one particular moment, but I am certain that your favorable service for your people continued well after you petitioned the king and advocated for your people. We know one person cannot be everywhere doing everything all the time. So thank you for showing us that, whether we are in the palace or the workplace, others help us to take note and pay attention to what they know and what they say without engaging in the gossip about it.

Queen Esther, my name may or may not get mentioned in the royal chronicles; however, I too was born for such a life as this. So far, I have not been called on as the one to save an entire nation of people. However, I have been allowed on many occasions to put on my finest apparel and host special feasts and gatherings to help celebrate and honor special people and reach out to individuals one at a time; I have also been allowed to lend support and encouragement or to help others navigate through a crisis.

When these situations arose, I, like you, had to take a decisive role for my own future and the future of a small band of my ilk. It was not until I had to step up that my old quietness and shyness fell away, so assertiveness could show up. There were many examples around me, including yours, that allowed me to evolve and call up these qualities when needed. Fortunately, when I needed wit and courage to come to the fore, I was not hiding behind my true identity.

I will keep the faith, I will remain assertive, and I will communicate in work, in business, and in play with the clout befitting our "queenship." This, my dear Queen Esther, is what allows me to celebrate my personal Purim, not annually, but as often as I need to.

Thank God for our sisterhood, Queen Esther. We have turned the tables and saved time and money, and we have seen success, promotion, and favor set up by our loving Father. As my journey continues, I pray to remain humble and ready to step up at the times when I am needed.

Dear Naomi,

I am sure you have even more stories that could have been told about the ups and downs of your life. We were allowed to take a look at the most significant one, which covers at least a decade or so, following the tragic loss of your husband and two sons. I empathize with the loss of your family. It seems your life was rich, abundant, and full, but then it appears that everything was taken away.

There was a famine in the land, and your husband thought it best to go where food was plentiful in Moab. After making that journey, the family decided to stay. It must have seemed very good, but then you became a widow. That was followed by the loss of both of your sons, your only children. They had reached adulthood and were married to two Moabite women. Now it was just you and your two daughters-in-law. You talked to them as a loving person would and told them to return to their first families. There were hugs and kisses before one said yes to returning home, while the other, Ruth, basically said that you were her family now. She had married into your family, and it was for life. She told you that she was not going anywhere except with you. Your people became her people, and your God became her God. She meant it.

With no male protector and provider in your immediate family, you decided it was best for you to return to your people in Bethlehem in Judah. It was time to sacrifice and uproot yourself again. This time it was different. When you had migrated before, you had a husband and two sons. Even so, you felt it was time to go. What helped you with that decision was knowing that God was helping the people of Israel.

You and Ruth went on your way. She clung to you. I am sure you appreciated her loyalty, support, and encouragement as you both stepped out with courage and faith. What followed, Naomi, was that you became a leader who had the foresight to send Ruth to the right place at the right time. In the process of setting all of this up to get family support and resources, you advised Ruth well and led her to God. You boldly set up the encounter between her and Boaz. You also instructed her on how to present herself to catch Boaz's eye. Yes, you did set it up, and after it was done, you were in a position to rest, because Boaz woke up. He went to his friends and the elders to settle a land deal from your inheritance from your deceased husband. (The culture at the time dictated that men should handle such matters.) Boaz made the deal and became the kinsman redeemer for both you and Ruth. He fell in love with Ruth and became her husband.

When you wanted to change your beautiful name from Naomi (which means "sweet," "pleasant," "joy," "bliss") to Mara (which means "bitter"), what we know now is that this was grief, mourning, and loss talking, which were most likely the predominate emotions overwhelming you at the time. You found enough strength to press on through the bereavement. That type of disruption to a pleasant life can be devastating. The importance of this piece of your recorded story is not about the circumstance, but about who you became in the situation. I know you were not mad at God, you just needed time to process your circumstances and formulate a plan.

I had a revolutionary turn in my life that was liberating. It didn't happen out of sadness or due to a specific situation; it was due to me being completely brand new and rebuilt. Once I started catching up on my correspondence, I noticed that this has been a theme: that when one's spirit emerges brand new, there is no sadness, pain, or regrets from the past. You like and appreciate all that you encountered on your path up to this very point, and there is so much new hope going forward, it is almost overwhelming. The sheer excitement of it is sometimes celebrated with a new name that better describes the new you. Although my situation is very different from yours, Naomi, I have an understanding of your need to reidentify yourself, even when it was only temporary. We can take nothing from the intensity of your personal inner feelings on that.

Your misfortune and heartache were God's illustration for us to see how he will bring something wonderful out of bitter circumstances. For our sake it may be necessary for us to be completely torn down to be rebuilt and better. God brought you from fullness to emptiness and back again. After Ruth's wedding you were bitter no more. You were restored. Boaz became your "new son" and your provider. You became grandmother to Obed, and great-grandmother to Jesse, and great-great-grandmother to King David. I would say you were restored, dear Naomi. Won't God do it?

Thank you that I have a lot of "Naomis" in my life who have shown me courage is one of the most valuable resources to get one from bitter to sweet.

Dear Ruth,

I am amazed at the way Naomi set things up for you! You were a good daughter and would not let her travel alone back to Bethlehem in Judah. I am sure she appreciated your companionship and your support. While you both were grieving, you summoned up the courage to start over. You had lost your husband, your brother-in-law, and your father-in-law, and she had lost her husband and her two sons—three members from the same family in such a short period of time. There you and Naomi were, with no male relatives to protect you and provide for you. Naomi stepped in and taught you about faith and led you to her God.

When you arrived, you had the wherewithal to know you could not just hang on to Naomi and look to her for provision. You took the initiative and went straight to the field to work the harvest to get what the two of you needed to survive. Naomi endorsed your decision. You were in a foreign place, and you went to work and demanded nothing. This had to take a lot of restraint and courage.

Ruth, I believe you would have been all right with or without Boaz. But we all know that that was not part of the plan orchestrated for your life. Boaz initially came to know of you by your reputation. He was a relative of your father-in-law, making him a kinsman to Naomi. He heard about how kind you had been to Naomi, and he said he would help you out because you were her companion and care provider. You supported her with no expectation of reward. Loyalty to your friends and loved ones is a real treasure. Boaz said you were to have food to eat, fresh water, and plenty of wheat and barley from the harvest to take to the marketplace for other provision for yourself and Naomi. Thus, you learned to barter and trade like a businesswoman. Boaz said you would be blessed by the Lord God of Israel because of your tenderness and loving kindness toward your elder. From this conversation, the blessings were already flowing. Boaz gave you protection as you continued to work in the lush fields. Apparently, it was a good crop that year.

You showed us how it pays to listen to wise instruction from our elders, and you went to Boaz when Naomi instructed you to do so. You were open-minded and teachable.

Boaz was paying attention. He saw your sweet disposition and your grateful attitude. Things started stirring up for him as he saw more of your inner beauty and how it matched your outer beauty. Boaz realized he needed to step in out of family obligation and duty. He handled the business regarding Naomi's inherited land and became responsible for the two of you. To his delight, he made you his wife. Naomi lost the bitterness in her heart when you and Boaz became husband and wife. You received the favor of God. You were blessed to be the mother of Obed, the grandmother of Jessie, and the great-grandmother of King David, and on and on the generations went, straight to the bloodline of Jesus.

Both you and Naomi were restored, renewed, and rewarded by the blessings of the Lord because of your kindness and faithfulness, and your story will stand for eternity.

You, dear Ruth, are a great example of what can become of a teachable, open mind. You demonstrated how kindness, loyalty, and compassion for our elders bring rewards in God's time. These are the lessons I received from you. Thank you.

Dear God,

My letter to you is open and living. I admire your for your matchless greatness, and I thank you for the life I am living right here and now. Thank you for all of the letters I have just written, because you placed all of those wonderful people in my life. I have been able to gird up and mount up a few steps toward the likeness of all of those to whom I have just written, out of admiration. They modeled something wonderful for me to strive toward.

Oh God, "The Bible is a book of faith, and a book of doctrine, and a book of morals, and a book of religion, of special revelation from *You*; but it is also a book which teaches man his own individual responsibility, his own dignity, and his equality with his fellow-man" (Daniel Webster [1782–1852] speech, at Bunker Hill Monument, 1843).

I love you, God, and I trust your holy book.

AUTHOR'S NOTE

THE LETTERS THAT WERE NEVER Sent is a collection of letters to people whom I admire and whom I believe have had an impact and a great influence on my life. I made the choice to share these letters as I was once again taking an inventory of what is in my heart and how it got there. Many of the included letters could not be sent because the person addressed is no longer living. (Some of the people addressed in *The Letters* were deceased before I knew of them and others were not even alive during my lifetime, yet others I never personally knew.) Still, I firmly believe I should "withhold not good from those to whom it is due, when it is in the power of thine hand to do it" (Proverbs 3:27). Therefore, I hope that by sharing the*se letters, I might positivel*y influence readers and give them new insight about some people I have admired in my past. Because of the powerful legacy these persons left behind, my life received enrichment, and I want to pass this on. Even though I could not send these letters, there are readers who may benefit from the beauty of how special, near, and dear the relationships remain in my heart, whether the person is on earth or not. I wish that we all may be prompted to speak the kind words of admiration and appreciation sooner to those we hold dear.